What Kids Are Saying About

The Mouse, the Monster a...

"Thanks, grandma. These books help me be a better kid." —11 year old Andrew

"I used to be a mouse and now I'm assertive." — Jennifer

"The crash course in school made me assertive instead of a monster." — Rick

"I guess at times I can be a mouse or a monster but hopefully I can live the rest of my life like an assertive person. What I liked best was 'How to Say No.' I think that will help me out a lot when I get into Junior High and High School." — Ashley

"Now I know how to be assertive and to say "no". I also know how to give compliments. Thank you for inventing this. I really appreciate it." — Nisha

"I learned that I have a lot of things that only I am in control of, like what I do at school, how I do my homework, and if I'll get a good job or not." — Brian

What Grown-ups Are Saying About
The Mouse, the Monster and Me

"A valuable and empowering book."

—Michele Borba, Ed.D., author of 22 books including *Thrivers* and *The Big Book of Parenting Solutions*

"The Mouse, Monster and Me teaches healthy non-violence conflict management skills that are more vital than ever in today's increasingly interdependent society."

—*Midwest Book Review*

"This simple, clever, and inspiring book can also help adults who are working toward healing old childhoodwounds. I highly recommend it for everyone—including teachers and therapists who help empower others!"

—Trina Swerdlow, Clinical Hypnotherapist, author of *Stress Reduction Journal*

"My son gave the book the best endorsement: 'You know that book about the monster and the mouse, Mom?' He smiled into the sun. 'It's like it was written just for me. How did the author know I struggle with stuff like this?' I wiped away a silent tear. Inwardly I thanked Pat Palmer for filling my little boy's heart with all the joy he deserves."

—Christine Louise Hohlbaum, author of *The Power of Slow*

"The Mouse, the Monster and Me tells how a person can learn to be ME. It is not good to be a Mouse and let everyone walk all over you. It is not healthy or wise to be a Monster and attack those who disagree with you. It is wonderful and secure and happy to be ME — non-threateningly assertive in positive ways that encourage others also to be themselves. If everyone lived by the lessons in this little book, there would perhaps be no wars, crime, or divorce! The lessons are that powerful."

—Bonnie Neely, Amazon Reviewer

"The Mouse, the Monster and Me is a must-have book for every parent and teacher! My children learned how to handle themselves in situations where they felt overwhelmed or enraged."

—Janet, Fort Wayne, IN

"This is my go-to book for helping children grow strong from the inside out. No other book matches this book in engaging children to claim personal responsibility for their words and actions, and in the process, becoming self-confident pre-teens."

—Penny, Elementary School Counselor

The Mouse, the Monster and Me
a Me Myself I book

Text © Pat Palmer 1977
Revised with Louise Hart, Ed.D. 2010
Images Copyright © Sue 2018
All rights reserved

Uplift Press
Oakland, CA
www.upliftpress.com
download teaching guide at upliftpress.com/teaching-guides

ISBN: 978-1-64704-551-7

Uplift Press plants a tree for every ten paperbacks sold.

iv

The Mouse, the Monster and Me:

Assertiveness for Young People

By Pat Palmer, Ed.D.

Illustrated by Sue Ramá

Dedication

This book is dedicated to children
who wish to be free and to the adults
who will help them.

To the Young Reader

This book is full of ideas about how you can grow up to be assertive, make good decisions and stand up for yourself. There are games for you to play to help you learn about yourself and new ways of thinking and expressing yourself. It is a good idea to practice each kind of assertiveness in this book with a friend or a parent or a teacher, so they can help you look and sound just the way **you** want to.

Pat Palmer

Contents

PART 1

About the MUSE the MNSTER and OU!

1

This book is not really about mice
... or monsters.
It is about YOU, however ...
and how you sometimes act like
like a mouse
... or like a monster.

And ... it is about how you can be
less like a mouse
... or less like a monster,
and ... be more like

YOU!

2

Mice can be nice. And people who act like our friend mouse are sometimes so nice that they allow themselves to be

walked on

doormat

by other people.

And sometimes . . . mice get

squashed

Some words people use to describe this kind of mouse are . . . shy, timid, afraid, passive . . . unassertive.

Monsters, on the other hand, (actually you probably prefer not to have a monster on either hand!) are seldom friendly or thoughtful or nice.

You may have known some nice monsters, but people who go around acting like monsters are the ones who step on nice mice.

Usually "people monsters" aren't much fun to have around.

Some words people use to describe "people monsters" are . . . bully, mean, pushy, aggressive.

Of course, all people are not

mice . . . or MONSTERS

Most are just themselves.
. . . Friendly
. . . Honest
. . . Thoughtful
. . . Fun to be with.

You probably are, too, but we can all learn to be better
and to like ourselves more.

5

You'll find in this book some good ideas about how to be yourself.

Strength and Power

Rights and Responsibilities

Asking for What You Want

CRITICISM

Compliments

Being Yourself!

PART 2

Your Strength and Power

You have strengths and power . . .

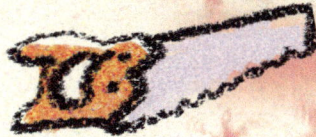

you may not even know about.

7

Every person has strengths,

talents,

abilities,

GIFTS

and . . .

SPECIAL

qualities.

Some are good in school. Some play ball well.
Some can draw and paint.

On a separate piece of paper, list your strengths.

8

Did you remember strengths like . . .

cooking

. . . singing . . .

building models . . .

working hard at a job

. . . listening carefully

. . . being a good friend?

(You can see that this kind of strength is not the same as **MONSTER** uses to push others around.)

Can you think of any more?

Everyone has an inner strength, too, which we can call POWER.
The monster confuses this POWER with acting TOUGH,
but that's not what it is.
The mouse gives away this POWER by letting other people make
the decisions which mouse should make.
POWER is the ability to be in charge of your own life.

Write down some examples of how you can be in charge of
your own life without pushing others around.

STRENGTH and **POWER**
grow when you use them.
As you grow up, you gain
strength and power
. . . to make more choices and
decisions for yourself . . . to be
more in charge of your own life.

By the time you are an adult . . .
you will know how to make good
choices and smart decisions,
and . . . you will be ready to be
on your own.

11

You can start right now by learning how to make choices.
Every person has choices of ways to act.
Sometimes you choose to do what you want to do.
Sometimes you choose to do what others want you to do.

Sometimes it is hard to
make up your mind.
When that happens you
can take a few minutes
. . . say to yourself,
"Relax."

RElaX

Close your eyes. Take deep breaths and feel calm.
When you feel calm . . . you can make choices more easily.

12

When you are relaxed and calm, use your strengths and power
...to make choices for you
...to make your life more the way you want it.

Do my homework
or play?

Clean my
room or
watch TV?

Tell Mom
I broke the
glass?

Report the
money
I found?

Go with the
group or do
what I want?

Play a trick
or be honest?

When you make choices and decisions for yourself,
you are being **assertive**.

Assertive may be a new word for you.
Being assertive just means you are letting . . . yourself and others
know what you want
. . . not in a **PUSHY** way like **MONSTERS** do
. . . or in a **scared** way like **mice** do,
but . . . in an honest way, just being

YOU!

Strengths Game

1. Sit in a circle with family members or friends.
2. Fold a piece of paper in half lengthwise. Put your name at the top of each side.
3. List your good qualities and the things you like about yourself on the left side.
4. Pass the paper to the person on your right. The person on your right lists the good qualities he or she sees in you on the right side.
5. Keep passing the papers until yours returns to you.
6. Compare the two sides.

Do people see me the same way I see myself?

How do I let others see more of my strengths?

Choice Game

1. Sit down with a friend or family member.
2. Start by each telling the other **5** things you HAVE to do. Such as . . . "I have to go to school." "I have to turn off the video game"
3. Now . . . say the same things and this time say, "I CHOOSE to . . ." instead of "HAVE to."
4. Share with each other how it felt to say, "HAVE to" and "CHOOSE to."

Which was easier to say?
How did your body feel when you said each?

I choose to. . .

16

What are you feeling right now?

PART 3
Your Rights and Responsibilities

Every person has rights and responsibilities.

I would like the right to own a pet, and I am willing to be responsible for taking care of it.

All persons have the right
. . . to be treated with respect.
Every person is valuable

regardless of

. . . size

. . . sex

. . . age

. . . race

. . . color,

language,

. . . or . . . religion.

20

The Golden Rule

"Treat others the way you want them
to treat you."

This is what being responsible means.
(It is also a good rule for being assertive.)

For instance:

... you borrowed something from a friend and broke it

... you're angry at your brother and are having an argument about whose turn it is to do the dishes.

What would ... a **mouse** say?

... a **Monster** say?

... an assertive **YOU** say?

All persons have the right . . . to be treated fairly.

Customer
Service

That means you have the right . . . to <u>ask for fair treatment</u> . . . and to <u>stand up for yourself in an **assertive** way</u>, if you are treated unfairly.

23

Everyone has the right . . . to express feelings . . . thoughts . . . and opinions. However . . . this right needs to be used in a fair and responsible way.

It is **NOT** OK to act like a **MONSTER** . . . and . . .

to put others **down** in order to express yourself.

For instance . . .
a discussion or even an
argument is OK, but . . .

SHOUTING someone down is **NOT** OK.

All persons have a right . . .
to be free from danger,
violence,
and harm.
No one has the right to
harm another.

You have a right and a responsibility . . .
to let other people know . . .
what you need or want.
No one can read your mind, so don't keep
quiet like a mouse!

Monsters tell people what they
want too loudly!

I WANT A
RED BIKE!
I WANT A PET
RACCOON!

You have a right to express your opinions and ideas about your own life . . . and . . . make more and more decisions as you grow older and more responsible. Such as . . . choosing your own friends, deciding what clothes to wear . . .
and eventually . . .
buying your own things.

Write down some decisions you would like to make for yourself.

How might you go about asking for permission to make these decisions?

(Hint: NOT like a m🐭use.

NOT like a M🧟NSTER!)

How do you think your parents or teacher or other adults will respond to this request?

Make a list of some of the rights you would like for yourself.

Your may wish to share this list with your parents. Perhaps together you can decide which rights you can have now, and which ones you can have when you are older.

1. I would like to be able to listen to the music I like.

We have a responsibility to do the right thing . . .

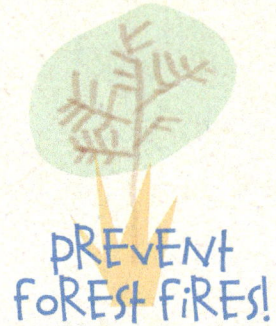

don't litTER!

No SMOKING

saVE ouR RiVERS!

PREVENT foREst FiREs!

. . . because we are members of a group, a family, a school, a class, a community, a country . . .

a woRld

List some of your responsibilities because you are a member.

We also have a responsibility to respect other people.

30

Sometimes . . . _rights_ and _responsibilities_ don't agree.
At those times you have a hard choice to make.

Since I'm responsible for
my bike, I'll put it away in
a safe place before I go in
to read my book.

Those choices are part of being human.

Remember:
Your most basic right
is to be _yourself._

PART 4
Asking for What You Want

I need a hug!

There are good ways . . .

and bad ways . . .

. . . of getting what you want.

Stomp! Stomp!

A good way to ask is <u>straight</u> <u>out</u>.

"I need some help."

That is being honest and assertive.

Some monster ways are . . .

**having a tantrum,
sulking,
hitting,
shouting,
getting mad.**

Some mouse ways are . . .

hinting, begging,
whining, pouting,
crying.

When you use

muse

or

MNSTER

ways
to get what you want,

you feel bad

and so does everyone else around.

I would like to be your friend.

Asking for what you want . . . _assertively_ . . . is more likely to get you what you want.

Write down some of the things you would like to ask for using assertive language.

Practice, with a friend or family member, assertive ways to ask for the things you want. Remember . . . to stand or sit up straight, to look at the other person, to talk in a normal (not whining or shouting) voice, and to be honest and direct.

It's OK to ask for what you want.
(But don't expect to always get it.)

PART 5
Saying NO

Saying **NO** can be like giving yourself a present.

It gives you . . .
- Time
- Ownership
- Privacy
- Your body
- Self respect

Happy No Day!

NO!

You have a right to say "No" when people ask you to do something . . .
- Illegal
- Dishonest, or
- Against your beliefs.

Those are times when you should be

firm!

For instance . . .
. . . your friend wants to see the answers on your test paper
. . . some of your friends want to throw rocks at birds
. . . someone wants to hurt someone or start a fight.

No. I like birds.

No. You can't see my paper.

No. I don't believe in that.

40

It is also OK to say "No" sometimes...

- When you need to be alone
- Don't want to loan your things
- Don't want to see a scary movie
- Are busy with homework or chores,

  or

- Need to take a rest...

...except...

It is not OK to say "No"

if:

it is a responsibility,

a rule, or

. . . something you have agreed to do.

And . . . remember . . . how you say

no

makes a difference.

Treat others as you like to be treated.

Saying NO Game

Sometimes it feels funny just to say "No".

It helps to practice with a friend or family member.

Take turns asking favors of each other — just pretending. Let the answer always be, "No."

Try saying "No" in different ways. Share with each other how it feels to say "No."

Help each other learn to say "No" assertively — firmly but without hurting the other person.

Would you let me use your bike?

PART 6

Criticism

When you are young it seems a lot of people can criticize you.

Grow up!
Don't do that!
Lazy!
You're LATE!
Don't slouch!
Be a man!
Boys don't cry!
Girls don't chew gum!
Your room is a mess!

What are some of the things you believe
about yourself that are different from the
things people say about you?

People say I am . . .

I believe I am . . .

Parents sometimes tell us things about ourselves that they would like to be true. For instance...
"You are going to be a famous..."

swimmer

dancer

pianist

actor

tennis star

ball player

inventor

47

How do you feel when you are criticized?
Check (✔) the ones that apply to you.

O 1. Hurt

O 2. No one loves me

O 3. Embarrassed

O 4. Guilty

O 5. Rejected

O 6. Like a bad person

O 7. _____

What do you do when criticized?
Check (✔) the ones that apply to you.

O 1. Want to hide.

O 2. Want to fight.

O 3. Get mad and talk back.

O 4. Cry.

O 5. Want to cry and can't.

O 6. Try not to think about it.

O 7. _____

It's your fault!

Not mine.

We need to learn what criticism about us is real and what criticism is unreal . . . what criticism is meant to help and what criticism is meant to hurt.

For instance . . .

You left the key to your house inside the house and someone calls you, "so spaced out you would forget your head if it weren't nailed on."

Is that real or unreal?

Sometimes . . . criticism sounds like you are always wrong, or bad, or trouble, because people often exaggerate when they criticize.

50

Some criticism can be helpful.
Useful criticism tells us things about ourselves
... that bother other people, or ...
... cause them to dislike us, or ...
... get us in trouble.

Learn to listen to criticism
and to decide for yourself
whether or not ...
it is behavior ...
you choose to change.

When people criticize you,
and you do not agree,
it is O.K. to tell them.

If criticism seems
to be true, you can
agree with it and . . .
say what you are going
to do about it.

Try practicing with
a friend some assertive
ways to handle criticism.

You do have faults because you are human. But . . .
having a fault doesn't
mean that YOU are not OK.

IT IS OK TO NOT BE PERFECT!

Nobody is! You can like yourself, and let yourself be OK, even though you still want to change some things.

After all, change is part of growing up to become the person YOU want to be!

When you are being criticized . . .

1. PUT ON ARMOR. Imagine yourself wearing armor, an invisible cape, or anything you wish to keep criticism from hurting.

2. STAY RELAXED. Take deep breaths, say to yourself, "Relax" and imagine yourself in a safe place for a few seconds if you start to get anxious.

3. DECIDE WHAT YOU BELIEVE. You don't have to believe every statement made about you. You can choose to accept or reject criticism. You are the world's foremost expert on the subject of you!

If you want to answer criticism, you can . . .

1. . . . agree. You could say, "Yes, I do that sometimes."

2. . . . disagree. Say, "No, I don't agree that I am lazy." Or, "No, I am not dumb."

3. . . . give yourself a compliment. "No, I am not dumb. As a matter of fact, I am quite intelligent." Or "I know that bothers you, but I really like myself." 4. . . . say nothing.

5. . . . say, "Yes, that is a problem for me, and I am working on it."

6. . . . say you would like to think about it and discuss it again later.

PART 7
Compliments

A compliment is like a gift.
Accepting it nicely
is being kind to the giver.

Both the giver and receiver
get warm feelings.

An honest compliment is not the same as "flattery."

A compliment is given freely, without expecting anything in return.

You sure did a good job with this.

You're so smart! Do you want to do my homework for me?

Flattery is like a bribe ... given to get something back.

When someone gives you a compliment, what do you feel and think? Check (✔) the appropriate ones.

○ 1. Wonder what to say.

○ 2. Feel warm and close to the person.

○ 3. Feel happy.

○ 4. Think the person is lying.

○ 5. Feel guilty.

○ 6. Wonder what they want from you.

○ 7. _____

- Which are mouse, monster, or . . . assertive ways of feeling?

When someone gives you a compliment how do you act?
Check (✔) the ones you do.

◯ 1. Blush and act embarrassed.

◯ 2. Pretend you didn't hear it.

◯ 3. Smile

◯ 4. Give a compliment back.

◯ 5. Put yourself down.

◯ 6. Look pleased and say, "Thank you."

◯ 7. Pat yourself on the back and say

   "Yes, I am the best."

◯ 8. Look at the floor.

• Which ones would you call . . . monster, mouse, or assertive ways of acting?

You can let the compliment in.
Say "Thank you," and smile.
Feel the warmth. Let yourself feel good!
Let the compliment all the way in to your body.
Let it give you warm, happy feelings.

Hold onto this nice feeling
as long as you can.
Remember the compliment, and . . .
say it over to yourself often.

Learn how to <u>give</u> honest compliments, too.

Let the people in your life know . . .

. . . you appreciate them.

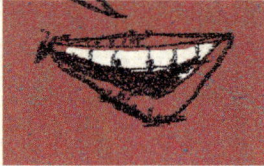

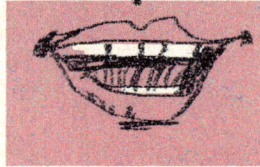

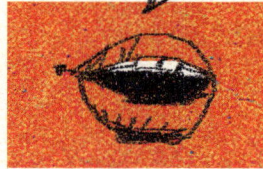

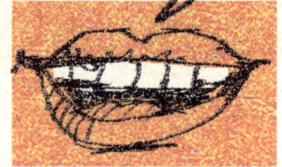

I enjoy being with you!

Thanks for the good dinner, mom.

That was really great!

I like what you did!

On a separate piece of paper write down some compliments you might give to the important people in your life. (sister, brother, mother, father, friends, grandparents, teachers, etc).

An honest compliment is a nice gift!

Accepting a compliment doesn't mean you owe something back in return.

I like your shoes!

Thanks! I like them too!

Giving a compliment doesn't mean the other person owes you something.

There are no strings attached to an honest compliment.

When you are feeling down
"take out" your compliments
and go through them slowly.

Or . . .

give an honest compliment
to someone else.

Either way . . . you will feel
better . . . fast!

The Compliment Game

1. Sit in a circle with your family or friends.
2. Have one person sit in the center.
3. Each person gives an honest compliment to the one in the center.
4. The person in the center should let the compliment sink in and say nothing.
5. After everyone has given a compliment, the person in the center returns to the circle, closes his or her eyes and remembers each compliment.
6. Each person takes a turn in the center.

66

PART 8
Being Yourself

Being yourself means that you are
willing to be in charge of your
own life
as you grow older.

When you accept more responsibility for yourself,
no one else has to "take care" of you.
That is being assertive and free in a very important way.

For Instance . . .

if you decide you will
take the bus or ride your bike *
rather than ask someone to drive you,
you are more free to come and go.

*after getting permission from your parents, of course!

Other Examples

If you decide to make your own lunch and tell your mother that you no longer need her to make your lunch — you accept the responsibility for making it or buying it.

If you want to take lessons to learn to play the piano, ride a horse, dance, skate, do gymnastics, ski etc. — are you willing to work to help pay for these lessons?

Write down some areas of your life where you could take charge.

Would you really like to be responsible for these things? Would other people let you be in control? Could you talk assertively to the powerful people in your life about taking control without upsetting them?

When you are assertive and responsible
for yourself others can't control you . . .
as they do mouse.

Others can't make decisions
for you.

Others can't force you to do
anything against your will . . .
as monster may try to do.

You are free to be yourself!

What are some of the things about your life you
would change if you could? Could you be assertive and
change these things by taking responsibility?
Write down some of them.

How would your parents, friends, and teachers feel
about your changes? Would they like you to take
responsibility for more things?

Some ways of being yourself are . . .

. . . To learn to like yourself.

. . . To be honest with yourself and others.

. . . To talk about your feelings.

. . . To give up your MONSTER ways of trying to control others.

. . . To give up your mouse ways of allowing others to control you.

. . . And . . . to practice being assertive like our assertive me.

Being assertive and being yourself means . . .
you know what you want and don't want . . .
(most of the time);
you can create your own opinions, beliefs and
ways to act; you can become free
by being responsible, by making good
decisions and choices.

You can be in control
of your own life.

Enjoy being **yourself!**

If you liked this book, you'll love...

Liking Myself

This fun-filled, charmingly illustrated book is full of ideas and exercises to improve self-esteem and assertiveness, and build emotional literacy.

Children learn to listen and to talk about their feelings. They also learn how to handle themselves when they feel upset or overwhelmed by encouraging them to write or draw their responses to specific scenarios.

"Valuable resources for building self-esteem and emotional stability. Highly recommended."

– Midwest Book Review

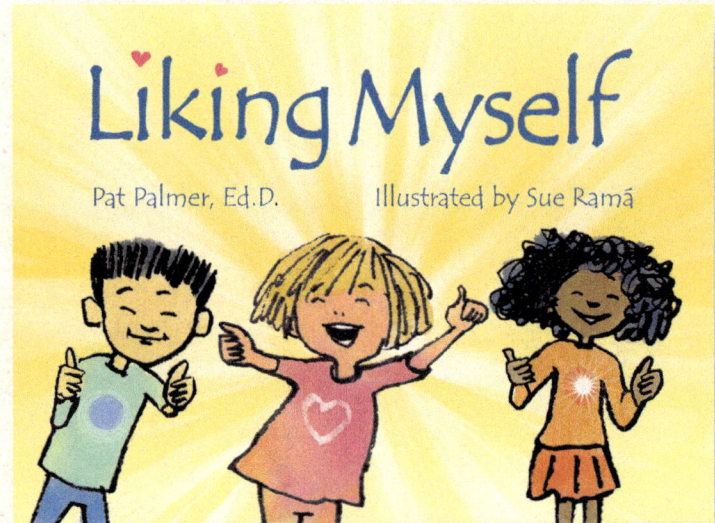

Liking Myself

Pat Palmer, Ed.D.   Illustrated by Sue Ramá

ISBN: 978-1-64704-549-4

a MeMYSeLfi book

What people have been saying about
Both Books

"Dr. Pat Palmer's two self-help books for children and young adults serve as excellent tools for teachers, therapists, and parents. Both titles are highly recommended."

—*Midwest Book Review*

"Pat Palmer has the gift of speaking to and for children. In a time when children are bombarded on all sides by destructive media messages, Dr. Palmer helps children understand the value of kindness and caring — including kindness and caring for oneself. She has the gift of speaking to and for children."

— Riane Eisler, author of *The Chalice and The Blade, Tomorrow's Children, The Partnership Way, The Real Wealth of Nations*, and others

"I have used these books for all of my 23 years of elementary counseling classroom lessons. My copies are tattered beyond repair. They are among the best resources to teach assertiveness and personal skills. Students retain the information and refer to them years later!"

—Marilyn Agee, M.Ed., LMHC,
National Counselor of the Year Award of the American School Counselor Association (ASCA)

"*The Mouse, The Monster and Me* and also *Liking Myself* help teach assertiveness at an early age. They help kiddos learn how to be responsible for their actions, words and feelings. Also, they help children learn how to deal with bullies."

— Lenore Webb

"These books are fantastic. I really enjoyed reading them myself, and I intend to use them in my work with juvenile offenders. Many read at the 3rd and 4th grade levels, and, unfortunately many do not like themselves."

—David, Parole Agent, Department of Youth Authority, Los Angeles, CA

"These books should be on a 'MUST READ LIST' for every parent and child on earth. They could change the culture!"

— Joseph

MeMYSeLf books

PERSONAL SKILLS FOR KIDS

Available in Spanish

El ratón, el **MONSTRUO** y **yo**

Conducta asertiva para los jóvenes

Por Pat Palmer, Ed. D.
Ilustrado por Sue Ramá
Traducido por María L. Villagómez

ISBN: 978-1-64704-639-2

Cómo apreciarme

Pat Palmer, Ed. D.

Ilustrado por Sue Ramá
Traducido por María L. Villagómez

ISBN: 978-1-64704-638-5

FREE Teaching Guides in English and Spanish

Download for free:
upliftpress.com/teaching-guides

Our free Teaching Guides provide lessons for each chapter, allowing students time to explore concepts in greater depth and gain a deeper understanding.

Principals, PTAs, non-profits, distributors and agencies can ask about discounts at: https://upliftpress.com/about/contact-us/

More from Uplift Press

Updated for a new generation

A hopeful, engaging guide to positive parenting that focuses on the personal growth and development of parents along with their children. It offers a new, hopeful model for families where everyone can feel like a success. Dr. Louise Hart's cherished classic has been updated by her daughter, Kristen Caven.

"Uniquely inspiring, accessible, and non-guilt-provoking!"

—Mothering Magazine

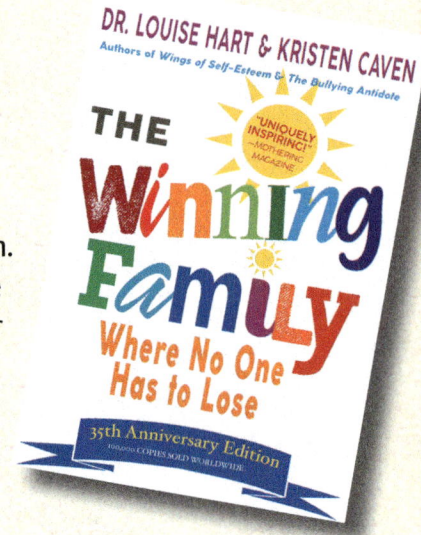

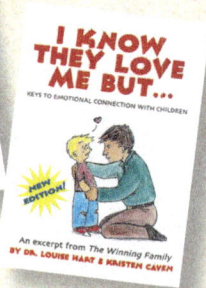

DR. LOUISE HART & KRISTEN CAVEN
Authors of *Wings of Self-Esteem* & *The Bullying Antidote*

THE
Winning Family
Where No One Has to Lose

"UNIQUELY INSPIRING!"
—MOTHERING MAGAZINE

35th Anniversary Edition
100,000 COPIES SOLD WORLDWIDE

NEW EDITION!
SELF ESTEEM:
THE BEST GIFT
for Your Children...and Yourself!

An excerpt from *The Winning Family*
BY DR. LOUISE HART & KRISTEN CAVEN

I KNOW THEY LOVE ME BUT...
KEYS TO EMOTIONAL CONNECTION WITH CHILDREN

NEW EDITION!

An excerpt from *The Winning Family*
BY DR. LOUISE HART & KRISTEN CAVEN

Free Excerpts

Visit www.upliftpress.com to get your free booklet.
Self-Esteem: The Best Gift for your Children AND Yourself! or
I Know They Love Me, But…

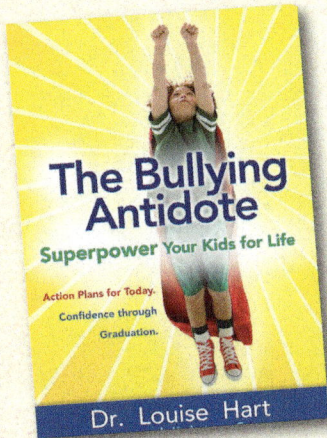

The Bullying Antidote by Dr. Louise Hart & Kristen Caven is a critical, life-saving book that gives parents the tools they need to break the cycle of bullying dynamics. Packed with insight and helpful information on how bullying relates to all societal ills, a resource for building deep connection, protection, and empowerment.

"Parents will find pointers to help kids who are being bullied, help kids who witness bullying, and even to intervene to help their child who is acting like a bully."
— Dr. Laura Markham, author of *Peaceful Parent, Happy Kids*

On the Wings of Self-Esteem, also by Dr. Louise Hart and Kristen Caven, shows how self-esteem is lost, how it is regained, and how to keep it.

"A wonderful book! If everyone read this book and did the exercises, half the pain and suffering we currently experience would disappear. "
— Jack Canfield, author, *Chicken Soup for the Soul*

Both books available at www.upliftpress.com

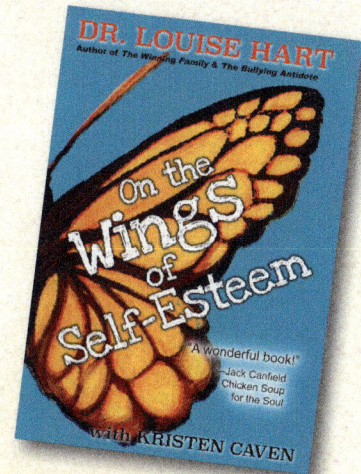

Printed in Great Britain
by Amazon